CURSIVE
WORKBOOK
FOR KIDS

This Book Belongs To

_____

Copyright © 2024

Importance Of
Cursive Handwriting

We firmly believe that the art and skill of cursive writing is both beautiful and important. We live in the digital age, but the most beautiful and important words are still written by hand.

There are many benefits to having cursive writing skills. Writing in cursive not only allows you to form words more easily but also helps in constructing better sentences. **It's proven that children who learn and write in cursive experience an increase in skills related to syntax.**

Cursive writing will also help you develop your unique signature. As an adult, you will need to sign important documents, and a handwritten signature is much more difficult to forge. Moreover, writing in cursive is faster than typing, making it an incredibly practical skill, especially in studying and test-taking scenarios. Additionally, it's undeniable that a handwritten letter holds more value and romance compared to one that is printed or sent by email.

It is also well known that play is the highest form of learning! That's why this workbook will guide you from the very beginning from learning how to write single letters, to joining them and forming short words, to eventually writing whole sentences in a fun and entertaining way.

Instead of rewriting boring sentences, you will practice with inspirational sentences. Rather than becoming bored from repetitive tasks, you'll engage in copying and creating your own funny sentences. And as a break, you can enjoy playing word games and fill in the blank! Sounds good, doesn't it?

About The Book

This workbook is designed to guide young learners through the intricacies of cursive handwriting, adhering to widely recognized standards with a consistent approach throughout. It's important to note that while much of cursive writing is objective, certain aspects remain subjective and open to stylistic preference. For example, in this book, we do not connect capital letters to their following lowercase letters, although it is possible to do so based on the writer's choice. Additionally, you may notice variations in specific letters, such as the capital 'Q'. We have selected one style for clarity and consistency; however, other variations exist and can be explored as each writer develops their unique cursive style. We encourage learners to embrace these nuances as they refine their handwriting skills and express their personal style.

Inside, the workbook is divided into four sections:

1. Letters: Detailed instructions and practice exercises for individual cursive letters.
2. Connecting Letters: Activities focusing on joining cursive letters to form words.
3. Words: Practice for writing complete words, including fill in the blank exercises.
4. Sentences: Creative prompts and quotes for writing complete sentences.

Interactive elements such as fill-in-the-blank exercises and matching games enhance engagement. A structured outline including an introduction, instructions, activities, and conclusion, ensures a comprehensive learning experience.

Overall, the workbook aims to provide an enjoyable learning journey for kids aged 8-12 to improve their cursive writing skills.

Tips and Tricks

1. Posture: Sit up straight with feet flat on the floor.

2. Grip: Hold pen lightly with thumb, index, and middle fingers.

3. Paper Angle: Tilt for comfort (left for right-handed, right for left-handed).

4. Basics First: Practice loops, curves, and lines before letters.

5. Consistent Slant: Maintain a slight forward angle to the right.

6. Regular Practice: Dedicate daily time to improve.

7. Slow and Steady: Focus on accuracy before speed.

8. Break it Down: Learn complex letters stroke by stroke.

9. Follow Guide: Use dotted lines and arrows in workbooks.

10. Review and Improve: Reflect on progress regularly.

11. Stay Patient: Progress takes time, so stay positive and persistent.

A SHORT MESSAGE TO YOUNG READERS

Unlocking the art of cursive writing is like discovering a new superpower within yourself! Every stroke of the pen is a step closer to mastering this elegant form of expression. Remember, every letter, word, and sentence you write is a testament to your growth and dedication. Embrace the journey, for with each practice session, you're sculpting a skill that will serve you for a lifetime. Believe in your abilities, stay persistent, and watch as your handwriting transforms into a work of art!

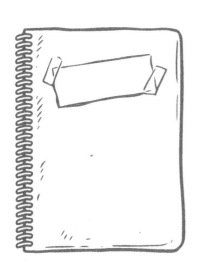

Part 1
Cursive Letters

Trace the dotted letters
Then write the letters on your own.

CURSIVE ALPHABET GUIDE

Aa Bb Cc Dd

Ee Ff Gg Hh

Ii Jj Kk Ll

Mm Nn Oo Pp

Qq Rr Ss Tt

Uu Vv Ww Xx

Yy Zz

Uppercase

a a a a a a

a a a a a a

a a a a a a

Lowercase

a a a a a a a

a a a a a a a

a a a a a a a

Uppercase

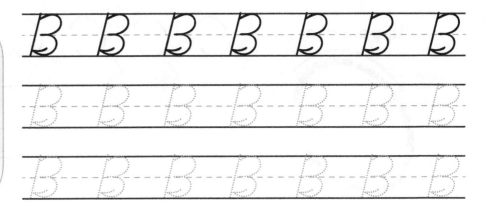

B B B B B B B

B B B B B B B

B B B B B B B

Lowercase

b b b b b b b

b b b b b b b

b b b b b b b

Uppercase

C C C C C C C

Lowercase

c c c c c c c

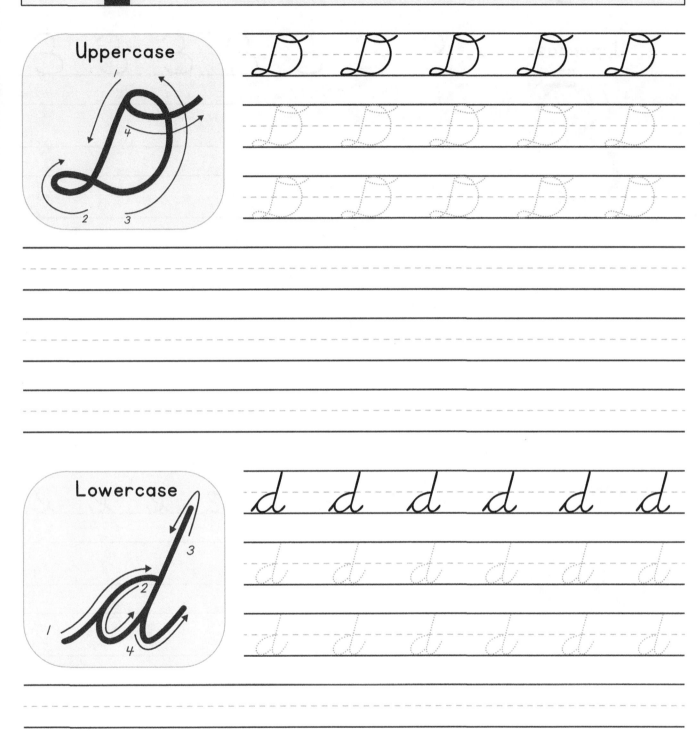

Uppercase

$\mathcal{D}$ $\mathcal{D}$ $\mathcal{D}$ $\mathcal{D}$ $\mathcal{D}$

Lowercase

d d d d d d

Uppercase

Ɛ Ɛ Ɛ Ɛ Ɛ Ɛ Ɛ

Lowercase

l l l l l l l l

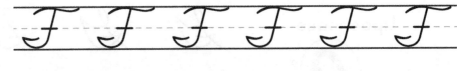

Uppercase

$\mathcal{F}\ \mathcal{F}\ \mathcal{F}\ \mathcal{F}\ \mathcal{F}\ \mathcal{F}$

Lowercase

$f\ f\ f\ f\ f\ f$

Uppercase

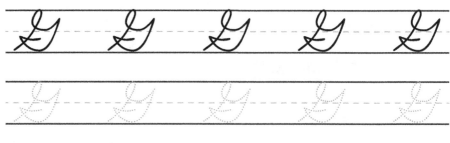

Lowercase

Uppercase

H H H H H H

Lowercase

h h h h h h h

Uppercase

Lowercase

Uppercase

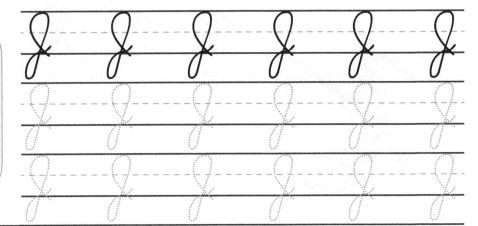

Lowercase

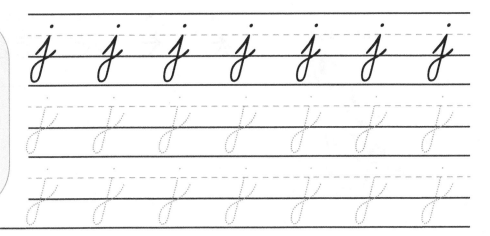

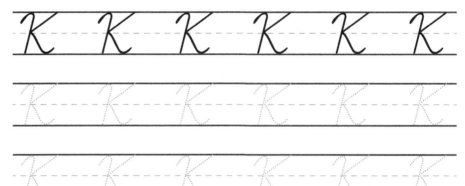

Uppercase

K K K K K K

Lowercase

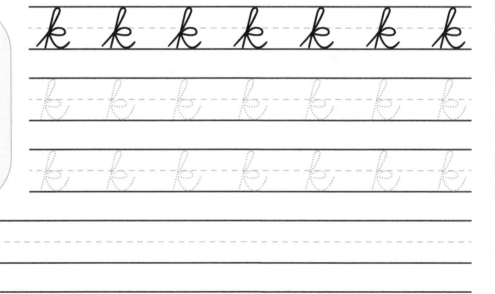

k k k k k k k

Uppercase

ℒ ℒ ℒ ℒ ℒ ℒ

Lowercase

ℓ ℓ ℓ ℓ ℓ ℓ ℓ ℓ

A B C D E F G H I J K L M N O P Q R S T U V W X Y Z

Uppercase

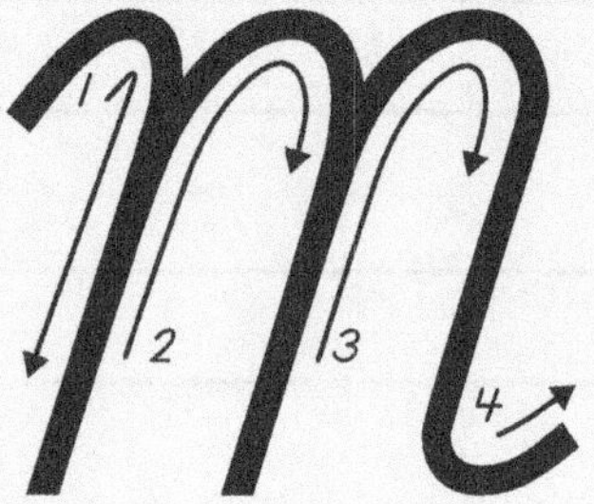

M M M M M

Lowercase

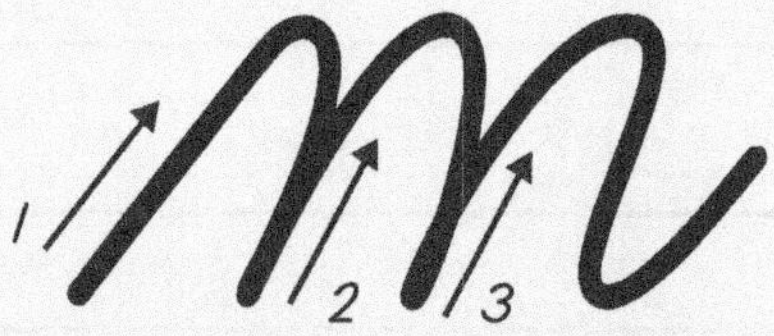

m m m m m

Uppercase

𝓃 𝓃 𝓃 𝓃 𝓃 𝓃 𝓃

𝓃 𝓃 𝓃 𝓃 𝓃 𝓃

𝓃 𝓃 𝓃 𝓃 𝓃 𝓃

Lowercase

𝓃 𝓃 𝓃 𝓃 𝓃 𝓃

𝓃 𝓃 𝓃 𝓃 𝓃 𝓃

𝓃 𝓃 𝓃 𝓃 𝓃 𝓃

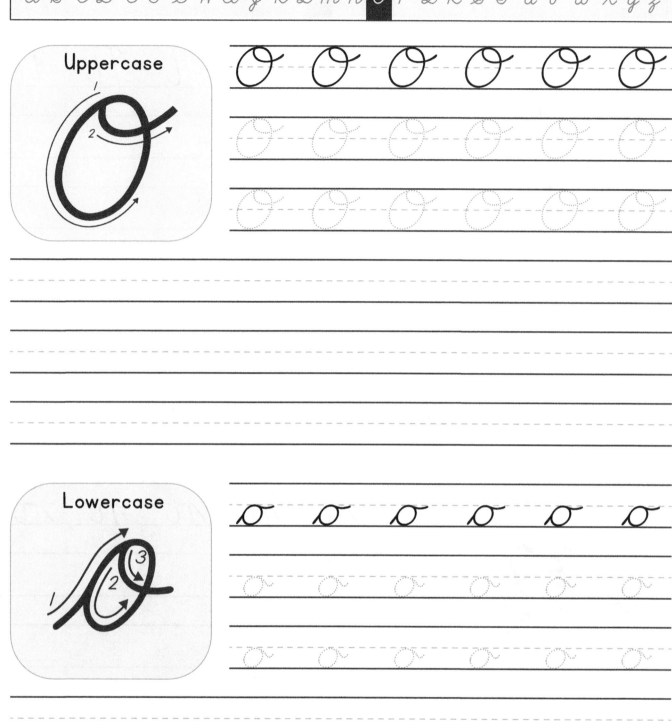

Uppercase

Lowercase

Uppercase

P P P P P P

P P P P P P

P P P P P P

Lowercase

p p p p p p

p p p p p p

p p p p p p

Uppercase

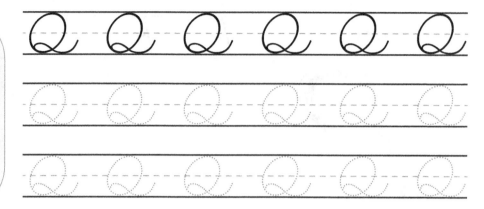

Lowercase

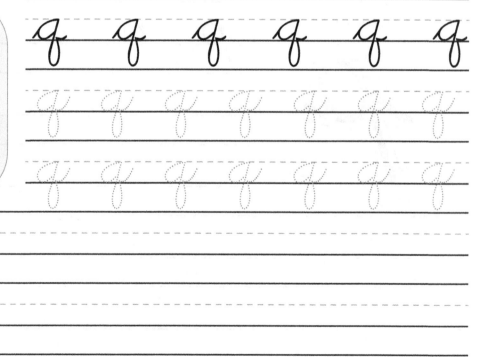

Uppercase

R R R R R R

R R R R R R

R R R R R R

Lowercase

r r r r r r r

r r r r r r r

r r r r r r r

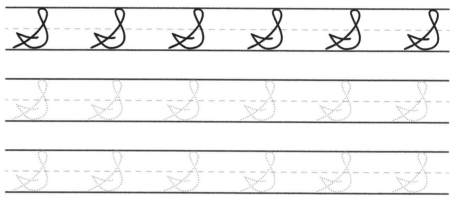

Uppercase

Lowercase

Uppercase

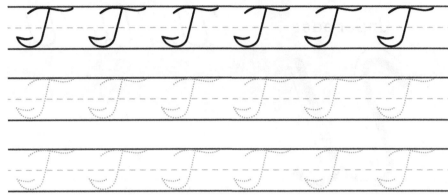

Lowercase

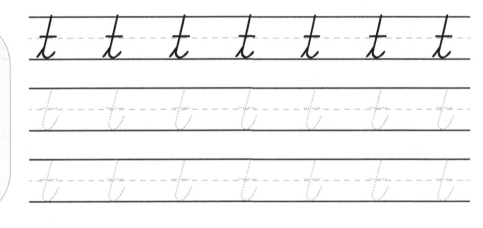

Uppercase

𝒰 𝒰 𝒰 𝒰 𝒰 𝒰

Lowercase

𝓊 𝓊 𝓊 𝓊 𝓊 𝓊

Uppercase

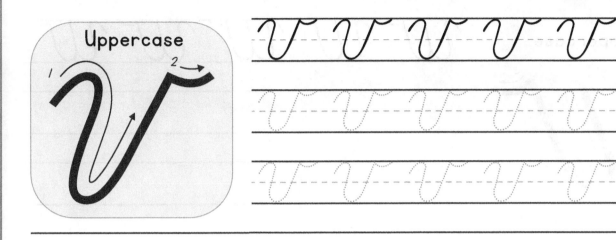

Lowercase

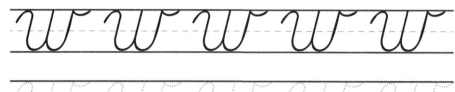

Uppercase

Lowercase

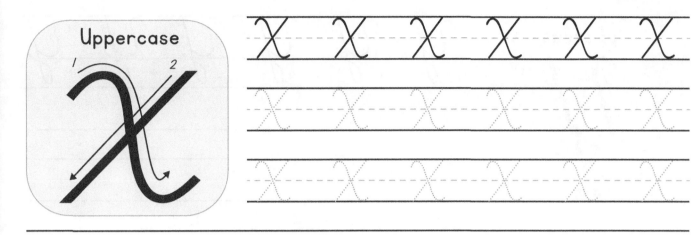

Uppercase

Lowercase

Uppercase

$\mathcal{Y}$ $\mathcal{Y}$ $\mathcal{Y}$ $\mathcal{Y}$ $\mathcal{Y}$ $\mathcal{Y}$

Lowercase

y y y y y y

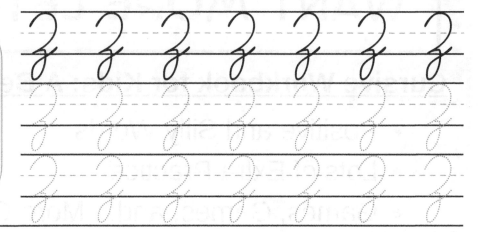

Uppercase

Lowercase

WANT MORE LETTERS?

Cursive Workbook for Kids: A Beginner's Guide

- Positive and Silly Words
- Lots of Extra Practice
- Games, Games, and... More Games!

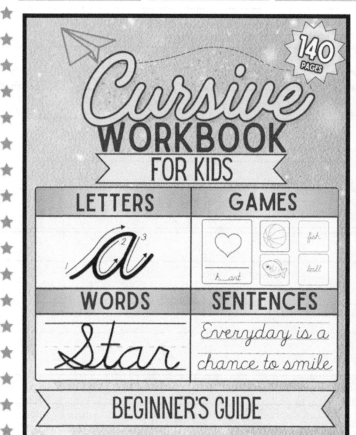

Part 2
Letter Connection
Practice

Trace the dotted words
Then write the words on your own.

Ay Ay Ay Ay Ay Ay

Ab Ab Ab Ab Ab

ae ae ae ae ae ae

af af af af af af

Bo   Bo   Bo   Bo   Bo   Bo

Bl   Bl   Bl   Bl   Bl   Bl

br   br   br   br   br   br

be   be   be   be   be   be

Cr   Cr   Cr   Cr   Cr   Cr

Ch   Ch   Ch   Ch   Ch

cl   cl   cl   cl   cl   cl

ca   ca   ca   ca   ca   ca

Dy   Dy   Dy   Dy   Dy

Dl   Dl   Dl   Dl   Dl

dk   dk   dk   dk   dk

de   de   de   de   de

Eg   Eg   Eg   Eg   Eg   Eg

Ej   Ej   Ej   Ej   Ej   Ej

em   em   em   em   em

eq   eq   eq   eq   eq

Fr   Fr   Fr   Fr   Fr

Fa   Fa   Fa   Fa   Fa

fc   fc   fc   fc   fc

fk   fk   fk   fk   fk

Gm Gm Gm Gm

Gr Gr Gr Gr Gr

go go go go go go

gs gs gs gs gs gs

Ho   Ho   Ho   Ho   Ho   Ho

He   He   He   He   He   He

hi   hi   hi   hi   hi   hi

hb   hb   hb   hb   hb   hb

ly   ly   ly   ly   ly

ls   ls   ls   ls   ls

ia   ia   ia   ia   ia   ia

it   it   it   it   it   it

PRACTICE CONNECTING TWO LETTERS

Ja   Ja   Ja   Ja   Ja   Ja

Jr   Jr   Jr   Jr   Jr   Jr

jh   jh   jh   jh   jh   jh

jb   jb   jb   jb   jb   jb

Kr   Kr   Kr   Kr   Kr   Kr

Ka   Ka   Ka   Ka   Ka   Ka

kn   kn   kn   kn   kn   kn

kp   kp   kp   kp   kp

Le   Le   Le   Le   Le   Le

Lo   Lo   Lo   Lo   Lo

lu   lu   lu   lu   lu   lu

li   li   li   li   li   li

My   My   My   My   My

Md   Md   Md   Md   Md

mh   mh   mh   mh   mh

mw   mw   mw   mw   mw

Nt   Nt   Nt   Nt   Nt   Nt

Ng   Ng   Ng   Ng   Ng

nf   nf   nf   nf   nf   nf

nb   nb   nb   nb   nb

Ov   *Ov*   *Ov*   *Ov*   *Ov*

Oi   *Oi*   *Oi*   *Oi*   *Oi*   *Oi*

og   *og*   *og*   *og*   *og*

ob   *ob*   *ob*   *ob*

Pe   Pe   Pe   Pe   Pe   Pe

Pi   Pi   Pi   Pi   Pi   Pi

ps   ps   ps   ps   ps   ps

pj   pj   pj   pj   pj   pj

Qe   Qe   Qe   Qe   Qe

Qh   Qh   Qh   Qh   Qh

gb   gb   gb   gb   gb   gb

gi   gi   gi   gi   gi

Rj   Rj   Rj   Rj   Rj   Rj

Ri   Ri   Ri   Ri   Ri   Ri

rz   rz   rz   rz   rz   rz

rb   rb   rb   rb   rb   rb

Sd   Sd   Sd   Sd   Sd

Sl   Sl   Sl   Sl   Sl

sc   sc   sc   sc   sc   sc

sr   sr   sr   sr   sr   sr

Tc   Tc   Tc   Tc   Tc   Tc

Ty   Ty   Ty   Ty   Ty

th   th   th   th   th   th

tu   tu   tu   tu   tu   tu

Ur   *Ur*   *Ur*   *Ur*   *Ur*

Uw   *Uw*   *Uw*   *Uw*   *Uw*

ug   *ug*   *ug*   *ug*   *ug*   *ug*

ui   *ui*   *ui*   *ui*   *ui*   *ui*

Vs   Vs   Vs   Vs   Vs   Vs

Vr   Vr   Vr   Vr   Vr   Vr

vg   vg   vg   vg   vg   vg

vk   vk   vk   vk   vk   vk

We   We   We   We   We

Wf   Wf   Wf   Wf   Wf

wb   wb   wb   wb   wb

wx   wx   wx   wx   wx

Xn Xn Xn Xn Xn

Xq Xq Xq Xq Xq

xl xl xl xl xl

xq xq xq xq xq

Yr   Yr   Yr   Yr   Yr   Yr

Yf   Yf   Yf   Yf   Yf   Yf

ye   ye   ye   ye   ye   ye

yw   yw   yw   yw   yw

Za Za Za Za Za Za

Zx Zx Zx Zx Zx Zx

zi zi zi zi zi zi

zt zt zt zt zt zt

Cry   Cry   Cry   Cry   Cry

Egg   Egg   Egg   Egg   Egg

ape   ape   ape   ape   ape

cab   cab   cab   cab   cab

Bar   Bar   Bar   Bar   Bar

Dot   Dot   Dot   Dot

elk   elk   elk   elk   elk   elk

hat   hat   hat   hat   hat

Fit   Fit   Fit   Fit   Fit

Gas   Gas   Gas   Gas

axe   axe   axe   axe   axe

ivy   ivy   ivy   ivy   ivy

Jam *Jam* *Jam* *Jam* *Jam*

Key *Key* *Key* *Key* *Key*

lap *lap* *lap* *lap* *lap*

mat *mat* *mat* *mat* *mat*

Mug   Mug   Mug   Mug

Nap   Nap   Nap   Nap   Nap

jog   jog   jog   jog   jog

yew   yew   yew   yew   yew

Rim Rim Rim Rim Rim

Sea Sea Sea Sea Sea

tag tag tag tag tag tag

urn urn urn urn urn

Vet   Vet   Vet   Vet   Vet

Web   Web   Web   Web

owl   owl   owl   owl   owl

keg   keg   keg   keg   keg

Pan   Pan   Pan   Pan   Pan

Rug   Rug   Rug   Rug   Rug

zed   zed   zed   zed   zed

vow   vow   vow   vow

Wig   Wig   Wig   Wig

Top   Top   Top   Top

pot   pot   pot   pot

mud   mud   mud   mud

Mud   Mud   Mud   Mud

Rat   Rat   Rat   Rat

yen   yen   yen   yen

zap   zap   zap   zap

Fill The Missing Letters

a__vent__re	yo__t__fu__
ex__e__lent	w__lli__g
v__r__atile	u__iqu__
und__rst__ndin__	ta__en__ed
s__nse	sm__ __t
r__spon__ibl__	qu__lit__
p__ayf__l	po__it__ve
pas__io__a__e	o__igi__a__

Answers: adventure, excellent, versatile, understanding, sense, responsible, playful, passionate, youthful, willing, unique, talented, smart, quality, positive, original.

Fill The Missing Letters

mot__v__ted

l__ve__y

lo__a__

ca__ef__l

kno__led__eab__e

j__yfu__

i__de__end__nt

h__ne__t

he__p__u__

g__at__f__l

ge__ui__e

f____rless

fr__en__ly

h__m__le

ex__lor__r

en__rge__ic

Answers: motivated, local, knowledgeable, independent, helpful, genuine, friendly, explorer, lovely, careful, joyful, honest, grateful, fearless, humble, energetic.

Write The Correct Name Under Each Item

Write The Correct Name Under Each Item

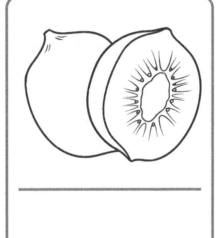

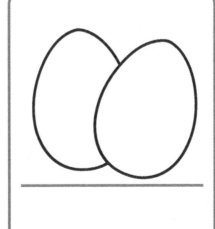

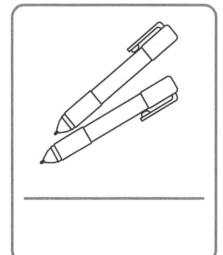

Write The Correct Name Under Each Item

_____

_____

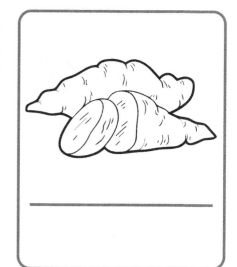

_____

_____

_____

_____

_____

_____

_____

WANT MORE CONNECTIONS?

Cursive Workbook for Kids: A Beginner's Guide

- Positive and Silly Words
- Lots of Extra Practice
- Games, Games, and... More Games!

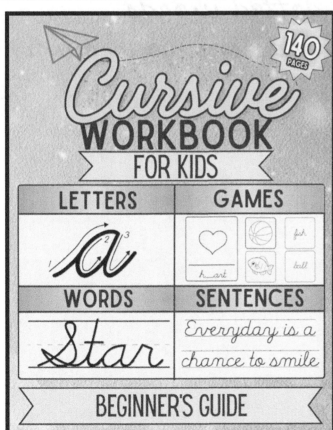

Part 3
Cursive words

Trace the dotted words
Then write the words on your own.

Amazing   Amazing

Adventure   Adventure

ambitious   ambitious

artistic   artistic   artistic

Brilliant   Brilliant   Brilliant

Brave   Brave   Brave

bookworm   bookworm

bubbly   bubbly

Creative   Creative   Creative

Curious   Curious   Curious

caring   caring   caring

confident   confident

Determined   Determined

Dynamic   Dynamic

dreamer   dreamer

daring   daring   daring

ABCDEFGHIJKLMNOPQRSTUVWXYZ

Energetic   *Energetic*

Empathetic   *Empathetic*

enthusiastic   *enthusiastic*

explorer   *explorer*

Friendly *Friendly*

Funny *Funny Funny*

fearless *fearless fearless*

free-spirited *free-spirited*

Genuine   Genuine   Genuine

Generous   Generous

go-getter   go-getter

grateful   grateful

Humble Humble Humble

Happy Happy Happy

helpful helpful helpful

honest honest honest

Imaginative *Imaginative*

Independent *Independent*

innovative *innovative*

insightful *insightful*

Joyful   Joyful   Joyful

Jovial   Jovial   Jovial

just   just   just   just

jocular   jocular   jocular

Kind-hearted *Kind-hearted*

Knowledgeable *Knowledgeable*

keen *keen* *keen* *keen*

kooky *kooky* *kooky*

Loyal   Loyal   Loyal

Leader   Leader   Leader

loving   loving   loving

lively   lively   lively

Motivated   Motivated

Mindful   Mindful Mindful

musical   musical musical

magnificent   magnificent

Noble   Noble   Noble   Noble

Nurturing   Nurturing

noteworthy   noteworthy

natural   natural   natural

Optimistic *Optimistic*

Open-minded *Open-minded*

outgoing *outgoing*

original *original*

ABCDEFGHIJKLMNOP QRSTUVWXYZ

Passionate Passionate

Positive Positive Positive

persistent persistent

playful playful playful

Quick-witted   Quick-witted

Quiet   Quiet   Quiet   Quiet

quirky   quirky   quirky

quality   quality   quality

Resilient   Resilient   Resilient

Reliable   Reliable   Reliable

responsible   responsible

radiant   radiant   radiant

ABCDEFGHIJKLMNOP2RSTUVWXYZ

Supportive   Supportive

Smart   Smart   Smart

spirited   spirited   spirited

sincere   sincere   sincere

Thoughtful *Thoughtful*

Talented *Talented*

tenacious *tenacious*

trustworthy *trustworthy*

Understanding *Understanding*

Unique *Unique* *Unique*

upbeat *upbeat* *upbeat*

unconventional

unconventional

Vibrant   Vibrant   Vibrant

Visionary   Visionary

valiant   valiant   valiant

versatile   versatile   versatile

Wise   Wise   Wise   Wise

Warm-hearted   Warm-hearted

witty   witty   witty   witty

willing   willing   willing

Xenial   Xenial   Xenial

expressive   expressive

exuberant   exuberant

excellent   excellent   excellent

Youthful   Youthful

Yielding   Yielding

yearning   yearning

yummy   yummy

Zealous   Zealous   Zealous

Zesty   Zesty   Zesty   Zesty

zany   zany   zany   zany

zestful   zestful   zestful

Fill In The Blank With Correct Words

1. The _____ jumped over the fence.

2. She found a _____ in the forest.

3. The _____ shines brightly in the sky.

4. After school, they went to the _____ to play.

5. He opened the door and found a _____

   waiting for him.

6. The _____ is the king of the jungle.

7. She wore a beautiful _____ to the party.

8. The _____ is filled with colorful fish.

9. They sat under the _____ and had a picnic.

10. The _____ was covered in snow.

11. She wrote her name with a _____ .

12. He packed his _____ for the camping trip.

13. The _____ was lost in the maze.

Answers: cat, treasure, sun, park, surprise, lion, dress, aquarium, tree, landscape, pen, backpack, explorer

14. She picked a _____ from the garden.

15. The _____ blew gently through the trees.

16. The _____ chased its tail in the yard.

17. She found a _____ inside the old, dusty box.

18. The _____ soared high above the mountains.

19. They rode their bikes to the _____.

20. He discovered a hidden _____ in the attic.

21. The _____ barked loudly at the mailman.

22. She wore a sparkly _____ to the dance.

23. The _____ glowed in the dark room.

24. They sat on the _____ and watched the sunset.

25. The _____ whispered secrets to the trees.

26. He found a lost _____ on the beach.

Answers: flower, breeze, puppy, treasure, eagle, beach, treasure, dog, gown, stars, bench, wind, shell

27. She built a sandcastle with a _____.

28. The _____ chirped happily in the morning.

29. They planted flowers in the _____.

30. He caught a big _____ while fishing.

31. The _____ hid beneath the bed.

32. She painted a beautiful _____ on the canvas.

33. The _____ howled at the moon.

34. They sailed across the _____ in a small boat.

35. He discovered a secret _____ in the garden.

36. She wrote a letter with a _____.

37. The _____ buzzed around the flowers.

38. They climbed to the top of the _____.

39. He found a treasure map in the _____.

40. The _____ rustled in the breeze.

Answers: bucket, birds, garden, fish, monster, picture, wolf, ocean, path, pen, bees, mountain, bottle, leaves

Writing Prompts - Answer Thoughtfully

1. What's your favorite color?

-

2. Describe your best friend.

-

3. Name a place you'd love to visit.

-

4. What's your favorite food?

-

5. Choose a word that describes your mood today.

-

6. Name an animal you find fascinating.

-

7. What's your dream job?

-

8. Select a word that represents your personality.

-

9. Describe your perfect day.

-

10. What's your favorite season?

-

11. What's your biggest fear?

-

12. Describe your ideal pet.

-

13. Name a hobby you enjoy.

-

14. Choose a word that describes your family.

-

15. What's your favorite book?

-

16. Describe your favorite holiday.

-

17. Name a goal you want to achieve.

-

18. Choose a word that describes your morning routine.

-

19. What's your favorite tv show?

-

20. Describe your dream home.

-

Match Words That Belongs Togather

Apple	Chair
Television	Pen
Table	Banana
Money	Remote
Paper	Staring
Car	Moneybag

Match Words That Belongs Togather

Bottle	Umbrella
Cycle	Rainboots
Rain	Easter Egg
Puddle	Water
Basket	Bird
Nest	Wheel

Match Words That Belongs Togather

Knife	Toothpaste
Bee	Key
Toothbrush	Fork
Bread	Sock
Lock	Hive
Shoe	Butter

WANT MORE PRACTICE?

Cursive Workbook for Kids: A Beginner's Guide

- Designed for Younger Kids, Ages 6-10
- More "Letters", "Connections", and "Words"
- More Games & Activities!

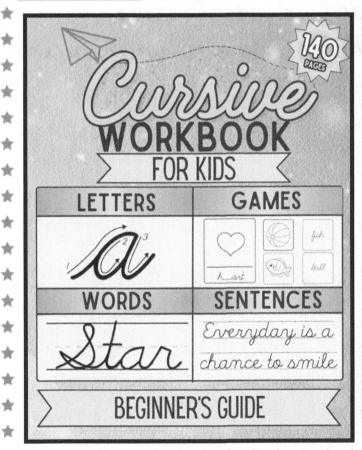

Part 4
Inspiring Sentences
Trace the dotted sentences
Then write the sentences on your own.

The only way to do great work is to love what you do. The only way to do great work is to love what you do.

Practice Time

When you know what you want, and want it bad enough, you'll find a way to get it.

When you know what you

want, and want it bad enough,

you'll find a way to get it.

When you know what you

want, and want it bad enough,

you'll find a way to get it.

Practice Time

We make a living by what we get, but we make a life
by what we give.

We make a living by what we
get, but we make a life by what
we give. We make a living by
what we get, but we make a life
by what we give.

Practice Time

How do we change the world ?
One random act of kindness at
a time. How do we change the
world ? One random act of
kindness at a time.

Practice Time

Strive not to be a success, but rather to be of value. Strive not to be a success, but rather to be of value.

Practice Time

You can't put a limit on anything. The more you dream, the farther you get. You can't put a limit on anything. The more you dream, the farther you get.

Practice Time

To succeed in life, you need two things: ignorance and confidence.

To succeed in life, you need two

things: ignorance and confidence.

To succeed in life, you need two

things: ignorance and confidence.

Practice Time

Keep your face towards the

sunshine and shadows will fall

behind you. Keep your face

towards the sunshine and

shadows will fall behind you.

Practice Time

Life does not have to be perfect to be wonderful. Life does not have to be perfect to be wonderful.

Practice Time

Life is a tragedy when seen in close-up, but a comedy in long-shot.

Life is a tragedy when seen in close-up, but a comedy in long-shot. Life is a tragedy when seen in close-up, but a comedy in long-shot.

Practice Time

There is only one success: to be able to spend your life
in your own way.

There is only one success : to be
able to spend your life in your
own way. There is only one
success : to be able to spend
your life in your own way.

Practice Time

When something is important enough, you do it even if the odds are not in your favor.

When something is important enough, you do it even if the odds are not in your favor.

Practice Time

I find that the harder I work, the more luck I seem to have.

I find that the harder I work,

the more luck I seem to have.

I find that the harder I work,

the more luck I seem to have.

Practice Time

Don't judge each day by the harvest you reap but by
the seeds that you plant.

Don't judge each day by the

harvest you reap but by the

seeds that you plant. Don't

judge each day by the harvest

you reap but by the seeds that

you plant.

Practice Time

Don't let yesterday take up too much of today. Don't let yesterday take up too much of today.

Practice Time

Gratitude is not only the greatest of virtues, but the parent of all others.

Gratitude is not only the greatest of virtues, but the parent of all others. Gratitude is not only the greatest of virtues, but the parent of all others.

Practice Time

If you really look closely, most overnight successes
took a long time.

If you really look closely,
most overnight successes took a
long time. If you really look
closely, most overnight
successes took a long time.

Practice Time

When you undervalue what you do, the world will
undervalue who you are.

When you undervalue what
you do, the world will
undervalue who you are.

When you undervalue what
you do, the world will
undervalue who you are.

Practice Time

If they don't give you a seat at the table, bring a folding chair.

If they don't give you a seat at the table, bring a folding chair.

If they don't give you a seat at the table, bring a folding chair.

Practice Time

Answer each question with a complete sentence.

What are the names of everyone in your family?

_____

- -

_____

- -

_____

- -

_____

- -

_____

What is your favorite breakfast food?

_____

- -

_____

- -

_____

If you could travel anywhere, where would you go and why?

_____

- -

_____

_____

- -

_____

Answer each question with a complete sentence.

What's the most exciting adventure you've ever been on?

_____
_____
_____
_____
_____
_____
_____
_____

Write about your favorite sport.

_____
_____
_____
_____
_____
_____
_____

What's your favorite thing about yourself, and why?

_____

_____

_____

_____

_____

_____

What's your favorite memory from a family vacation or outing?

_____

_____

_____

_____

_____

_____

Answer each question with a complete sentence.

What's the funniest joke you know?

_____
- -
_____
- -
_____
- -
_____
- -
_____

What's the coolest thing you've ever built or created?

_____
- -
_____
- -
_____
- -
_____
- -
_____

Answer each question with a complete sentence.

What do you enjoy doing the most during your free time?

_____
_____
_____
_____
_____
_____
_____

What's your favorite subject in school, and why do you like it?

_____
_____
_____
_____
_____
_____
_____

WANT MORE PRACTICE?

Cursive Workbook for Kids: A Beginner's Guide

- Designed for Younger Kids, Ages 6-10
- More "Letters", "Connections", and "Words"
- More Games & Activities!

    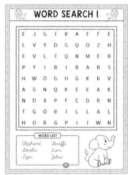

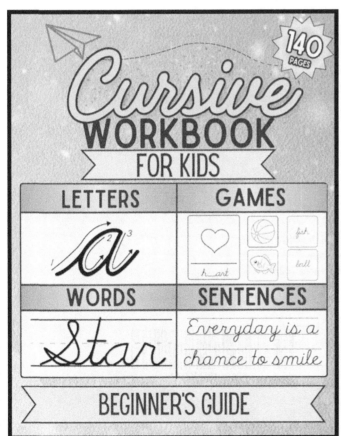

Made in the USA
Las Vegas, NV
30 September 2024

95962019R00077